Demonstrating Faith
In
Everyday Living

Non-Fiction

Sophie Allieu

Sierra Leonean Writers Series

Demonstrating Faith in Everyday Living

Copyright © 2017 by Sophie Allieu
All rights reserved.

No part of this book may be reproduced in any form or by any electronic or mechanical means except by reviewers for the public press without written permission from the publishers.

ISBN: 978-9988-8743-1-5

Sierra Leonean Writers Series
Warima/Freetown/Accra
120 Kissy Road, Freetown, Sierra Leone
Kofi Annan Avenue, North Legon, Accra, Ghana
Publisher: Prof. Osman Sankoh (Mallam O.)
publisher@sl-writers-series.org
www.sl-writers-series.org

CONTENTS

PREFACE ii

ACKNOWLEDGEMENTS iii

INTRODUCTION 1

ONE 4

   UNDERSTANDING FAITH 4

TWO .... Error! Bookmark not defined.0

   HOW DO YOU KNOW YOU HAVE FAITH? EVIDENCE OF

   FAITH .... **Error! Bookmark not defined.**0

THREE 43
   TEST OF FAITH - Faith in action 43
      BIBLICAL CASE STUDIES OF PEOPLE WHO
      PRACTICED FAITH 43
      REAL LIFE TESTIMONIES/LIFE EXPERIENCES OF
      PEOPLE WHO PRACTICED FAITH 48

FOUR 59

   GOD'S WORD AND PROMISES ON FAITH 59

FIVE 65

   BENEFITS OF HAVING FAITH 65

   HOW TO LIVE YOUR LIFE DAILY BY FAITH 67

ACKNOWLEDGEMENTS

I acknowledge my senior partner the Holy Spirit for the inspiration. Dr. Patrick George, my editor, who have been exceptionally supportive and motivational. Thank you my Publisher Osman Sankoh (Mallam O) of the Sierra Leone Writers Series for providing such an opportunity for writers to see their works published and of course for publishing this (my second) book. I keep counting.

May my God of answered prayers reward you all abundantly!

INTRODUCTION

The songwriter wrote:

> *"Through it all (2x), I've learnt to trust in Jesus, I've learnt to trust in God. Through it all (2x), I've learnt to depend upon his word.*
>
> *You know I thank God for the mountains and I thank Him for the valleys; and I thank Him for the storms He's brought me through. For if I never had a problem, I'll never know God can solve them. I never know what faith in His word could do."*
>
> **"Through it All" (Andrea Crouch)**

This book by the grace of God will be an eye opener, enlightenment to faith and for some it would be a refresher. So many people especially Christians use the word 'Faith' but some really do no fully comprehend what it is all about and how to put it into practice in their everyday living.

We should have an optimistic attitude at all times especially in bad times. A Christian should have a positive mindset. The realities and experiences of life seem to play tricks on our positive attitude, thereby leading to a shaky, wavering mindset.

People respond to negative situations differently:

Some lean on God's word. Others seek for spiritual strength and guidance through their religious leaders and fellow believers.

Others go to various prayer houses. Some even go to diviners, soothsayers, traditional healers, herbalist, fetish priests and the like.

There is also a set of people who believe that others are responsible for their predicament. Yes, they just blame others.

Certain people truly go through trials due to diabolical/satanic manipulation from Principalities, Powers, Rulers of darkness of this world and Spiritual wickedness in high places.

The works of witchcraft, agents of darkness, underworld, and fetish priest as a result of request from an enemy or wicked person could also be responsible for the negative things people face. Even Curses can be attributed to the misery people encounter.

There are those who give up, they allow the negative experiences they go through to get the better part of them, leading to serious health condition like high blood pressure. Some become insane and others even commit suicide or submit to the situation that kills them slowly until it finally claims their lives.

Demonstrating Faith in Everyday Living/Sophie Allieu

The demonstration of faith comes as we live our lives. It is not a one-off thing. Everyone can express or manifest faith differently under varied circumstances. The same person can have faith in God to heal a sick relative but that faith becomes weak or shaky when he/she becomes sick.

We cannot please God without Faith, because it is our show of faith that proves that we believe in Him. We believe first, that He exists and he is true without having proof or empirical evidence. God is happy when He knows we fully depend on Him and he will recompense us who persistently seek him.

God shows us his love, in tiny whinny ways at times. Ways we might not even notice. He always answers us just that we are so blinded by our imaginary and fantasizing expectations that we just don't notice His answers. Again, we don't receive answers because we are focused on how we want God to answer us.

He gives us the blessings He knows we can handle; sometimes testing us with little things: *"He that is faithful in that which is least is faithful also in much: and he that is unjust in the least is unjust also in much"*.(Luke 16:10 – KJV)

What you read here will not only elucidate but also open your heart's mind to understand faith as we live our everyday lives.

Prayer:

Heavenly Father, I pray for your spirit of understanding and enlightenment upon every reader. Let hearts be receptive, let lives be blessed through this book. Let people come to you. I pray that those who have backslide because of the problems they face in life will come back to you. Let the faith of your children increase and let your name be glorified. In the matchless name of our Lord Jesus Christ I pray, Amen!

Demonstrating Faith in Everyday Living/Sophie Allieu

ONE

UNDERSTANDING FAITH

According to Bible encyclopedia, **Faith:**
In the Old Testament (the King James Version) the word occurs only twice: Deuteronomy 32:20 (וּמֻא , 'ēmun); Habakkuk 2:4 (הנומא , 'ēmunah). In the latter the Revised Version (British and American) places in the margin the alternative rendering, "faithfulness." In the New Testament it is of very frequent occurrence, always representing πιστις, pistis, with one exception in the King James Version (not the Revised Version (British and American)), Hebrews 10:23, where it represents ελπις ,elpis , "hope."

The Biblical definition of Faith:

"Now faith is the substance of things hoped for, the evidence of things not seen." Hebrew 11:1 (KJV)

"It is important to notice that Hebrews 11:1 is no exception to the rule that "faith" normally means "reliance," "trust." There "Faith is the substance (or possibly, in the light of recent inquiries into the type of Greek used by New Testament writers, "the guaranty") of things hoped for, the evidence (or "convincing proof") of things not seen." This is sometimes interpreted as if faith, in the writer's view, were, so to speak, a faculty of second sight, a mysterious intuition into the spiritual world. But the chapter amply shows that the faith illustrated, e.g. by Abraham, Moses, Rahab, was simply reliance upon a God known to be trustworthy. Such reliance enabled the believer to treat the future as present and the invisible as seen. In short, the phrase here, "faith is the evidence," etc., is parallel in form to our familiar saying, "Knowledge is power."" (***Holy Bible - Bible Encyclopedia***)

The adage that says: "seeing is believing" does not apply here. With Faith, we hope that something will happen. For instance, when a woman is pregnant she hopes to be delivered of the baby. She also hopes that the baby grows up into an adult and becomes a personality she would be proud of. Her mind is always positive, thinking of the best. ***That is faith in action.***

The parents of the unborn child are already filled with joy at the fact that they are going to have a child. They think of what to do and make plans toward the coming of the child. Miscarriage, stillbirth, early childhood death etc. are not things they think about because they do not hope for such. We say they have faith because they are hopeful that the child will be born and safely at that.

"Yet, certain though the hope might be, it was not yet attained, and the interim was an opportunity to develop faith, *the substance of the things hoped for*. Indeed, hope is simply faith directed toward the future, and no sharp distinction between faith and hope is attainable. In particular, in Romans 8:24 *for in this hope we were saved. But hope that is seen is no hope at all. Who hopes for what they already have?* We have as the most natural translation, "By hope we were saved" On the other hand this steadfastness, produced by hope, reacts again on hope and increases it (Romans 5:4; Romans 15:4)."(**Holy Bible - Bible Encyclopedia**)

When we believe that something has happened even when we have not seen it happen, is also Faith. For example, you are trusting God for a job and you start thanking God for the job and go ahead to get your clothes ready for work.

"Evidence" is also the translation of elegchos, "conviction," in the King James Version of Hebrews 11:1, "Now faith is ... the evidence of things not seen," the English Revised Version "proving," "or test". The Greek word denotes "putting to the test," examining for the purpose of proof, bringing to conviction (Dr. W. F. Moulton). It is important to note the true nature of faith according to the correct translation of Hebrews 11:1, as being the well-grounded and assured conviction of things not seen." (***Holy Bible - Bible Encyclopedia***)

It is faith that makes the Elders of the church hear and gain favor from God to prevail, hold true on to the manifestation of God's power and acquire/possess the anointing to do exploit. *"For by it the elders obtain a good report"* Hebrew 11:2 (KJV)

It is by Faith that we understand creation because God did not use things to create things, like manufacturers do. He spoke and things came into existence. No one without faith can understand this, because it is only by faith that we believe. *"Through faith we understand that the worlds were framed by the word of God, so that things which are seen were not made of things which do appear."* Hebrew 11:2 (KJV)

According to offline English dictionary version 1.2.2, *Faith* is:

"1. A feeling, a conviction, or belief that something is true or real, without having evidence."

As Christians we do not see God physically under normal circumstances but believe in His existence and that He is the only true God and is real.

2. A religious belief system"

Most times, Christianity is referred to as "the Christian faith", "the Faith". When someone backslides, they say that individual has moved from or away from "the faith".

The Bible went on to say:

> *"But without faith it is impossible to please him: for he that cometh to God must believe that he is, and that he is a rewarder of them that diligently seek him."*
>
> Hebrew 11:6 (KJV)

We cannot please God without Faith, because it is our show of faith that proves that we believe in Him. We believe first, that He exists and he is true without having proof or empirical evidence. God is happy when He knows we fully depend on Him and that he will recompense us who persistently seek him.

Jesus, during His ministry on earth preached on faith.

"And Jesus said unto them, Because of your unbelief: for verily I say unto you, If ye have faith as a grain of mustard seed, ye shall say unto this mountain, Remove hence to yonder place; and it shall remove; and nothing shall be impossible unto you." (Matthew 17:20 – KJV)

"Jesus answered and said unto them, Verily I say unto you, If ye have faith, and doubt not, ye shall not only do this which is done to the fig tree, but also if ye shall say unto this mountain, Be thou removed, and be thou cast into the sea; it shall be done." (Mathew 21:21-KJV)

Jesus himself knew that our faith is not evident because of our doubt and unbelief. He encouraged all to show faith; for with even a little show of faith, which He tried to equate to that of a mustard seed (a small seed which is considered to be the smallest grain on earth) the impossible becomes possible.

By the revelation and inspiration of the Holy Spirit, I was abled to understand faith and I am going to define faith as God made me see it. The first step of faith is, believing in the word. There is a saying that goes like this: "what you believe is what works for you". The word is spoken and you believe in it no matter the prevailing condition you are in. For instance you are sick and in severe pain; an excruciating pain that you think will leave that part of your body abnormal or deform, if it is your foot, you wont be able to walk properly again; and the scripture that comes to mind is: *"... and by His wounds, we are healed" (Isaiah 53:5 - NIV)*. You say to yourself I feel pain right now but I believe in God's word that says I am healed; therefore, the pain will go.

Lets look at the NIV version of this scripture. *"Now faith is confidence in what we hope for, an assurance about what we do not see" (Hebrews 11:1)*. For the word to be made manifest in your life, you have to believe in the word. What you hope for is total healing. You hope that the pain will not only cease but also vanish for good. That is the confidence you have. At the moment in time, what you feel is pain but because the word of God says by His stripes you are healed you hope that, that word will come to pass in your life. That's the hope you have. To be healed, to experience total healing, and that the organ of your body that gives you pain will be normal and function well again. You believe that by His stripes you are healed but you do not experience healing at that particular moment but pain; but because you have assurance in His word that what He says He will do, His word is yea and amen. It is established. What He says will come to pass. He is not man that should lie, nor a son of man that needs to repent. That is the assurance you have that God is able to heal you. He has said it and He will surely do it. That is a show of your faith.

Believing is not just what gives the breakthrough that is why it is said that faith without works is dead. You have to go beyond what you believe. You hope, that the word spoken will be evident in your life and look forward to its manifestation.

So I define faith as cultivating an attitude that what you hope for, you get; and that which you want to see, you see.

Faith and Works

Faith as a word on its own is meaningless and useless. To say we have faith does not mean our faith is at work or can work for us. It is when our actions prove that we believe, trust and hope in God and that He will turn our bad situations to a good one; that is when we say we are exercising our faith.

When we say Works, we mean good works.

> *"What doth it profit, my brethren, though a man say he hath faith, and have not works? Can faith save him?"* **(James 2:14-KJV)**

The book of James chapter two verse seventeen confirms it all:

> *"In the same way, faith by itself, if it is not accompanied by action, is dead."* **(James 2:17-NIV)**

Let us examine the following scriptures in James 2:15-26 KJV:

> *"If a brother or sister be naked, and destitute of daily food, And one of you say unto them, Depart in peace, be ye warmed and filled; notwithstanding ye give them not those things which are needful to the body; what doth it profit?*
>
> *Even so faith, if it hath not works, is dead, being alone.*
>
> *Yea, a man may say, Thou hast faith, and I have works: shew me thy faith without thy works, and I will shew thee my faith by my works.*
>
> *Thou believest that there is one God; thou doest well: the devils also believe, and tremble.*
>
> *But wilt thou know, O vain man, that faith without works is dead?*
>
> *Was not Abraham our father justified by works, when he had offered Isaac his son upon the altar?*
>
> *Seest thou how faith wrought with his works, and by works was faith made perfect?*

> *And the scripture was fulfilled which saith, Abraham believed God, and it was imputed unto him for righteousness: and he was called the Friend of God.*
>
> *Ye see then how that by works a man is justified, and not by faith only.*
>
> *Likewise also was not Rehab the harlot justified by works, when she had received the messengers, and had sent them out another way?*
>
> *For as the body without the spirit is dead, so faith without works is dead also."*

Belief produces good works. **Faith** is the foundation and good **Works** is its fruit. Of what good is Faith if it does not produce love and justice for others?

It is said that everyone can do good works. We know people who do not believe in Jesus Christ but are Philanthropists supporting the education of poor children; adopting or serving as foster parents for Orphans; and there are some believers of Christ who do not even have the heart of kindness. Likewise, if a believer practices "works" without love, then it is not good works. Yes! There are times we do "good works" to show-off, to prove a point, to hurt those around us.

Counseling is one good works. Our positive attitude and behavior in Christ should show good works and subsequently our Faith as in the case of Noah:

When the rest of the world was wicked, Noah kept his integrity. God's good will towards Noah produced this good work in him. He was a just man that is, justified before God, by faith in the promised Seed. As such he was made holy, and had right principles; and was righteous in his conversation. He was not only honest but was devout. It was his constant care to do the will of God.

God looks down with an eye of favor upon those who sincerely look up to him with an eye of faith.
Works in the context of faith means, putting faith into action. In other words, it is the doing part of faith. What we do to show we have faith, to show we believe God can do it. Simply put, Works is how our ways of life serve as an evidence of our faith.

When we are in a situation where we seem to have no one to help or rescue us, when the going gets tough, yet we resist all temptations from the pit of hell and say we will wait on the Lord no matter how long; those around us may think we are wicked to ourselves or have given up. Some even think we are lazy, unserious or the hand of God is no longer upon us.

When God promises, He fulfills. His word is yea and amen. It will tarry for a while but will surely come to pass at the fullness of time. If God says He will supply your needs according to His riches in glory, He will.

Sometimes we make the devil so heroic. We glorify the devil by believing he is not only responsible for every negative thing we face, but has really succeeded in putting us in the position he wants us to be, like not affording to provide a square meal for your family because that business is not doing well or you have lost your job etc. That is the most ungodly thought any believer could have. The Bible says in Psalms 24: "The earth is the Lord's and everything in it, the world, and all who live in it". The devil has nothing. He is the prince of this world. Yes. But he does not own the world and everything in it.

So take your rightful place and exercise your authority through Christ Jesus to possess your possession because you are a hier, a bride of the Lord. ***Stop wallowing in self-pity and stop feeling defeated. Rise up! Take back what the devil has stolen from you through fasting; prayer/warfare, reading the word of God and above all believing you have overcome.***

The devil is a defeated fool. He plays on minds. He is a tricky thing. Know that you serve an all-powerful God, who created the very Lucifer (Formerly, the bright Morning star). Confess the word of God, take away fear from your mind and prove to the devil that greater is He (God) that is in you than he (the devil) that is in the world.

Characteristics of Good Works

I. Could be good works in words or deeds
II. Comes from the heart
III. We do it to glorify God and not oneself
IV. Are fruits of the spirit
V. We do it to appreciate and give thanks to God.
> *"And whatever you do, whether in word or deed, do it all in the name of the lord Jesus, giving thanks to God the Father through him."* – (Colossians 3:17 NIV)

What makes the good works of a believer different from that of an Unbeliever?
Lets examine this scripture: Acts 8:37
> *"And he orders to stop the chariot. Then both Philip and the Eunuch went down into water and Philip baptized him."(NIV)*

"Philip was directed to go to a desert. Sometimes God opens a door of opportunity to his ministers in very unlikely places. We should study to do 'good' to those we come into company with by travelling. We should not be as shy of all strangers as some are meant to come our way for specific purposes; if we know nothing of them, we at least we know they have souls. It is wise for men of business to make out time for holy duties, to fill up every minute with something that will turn to a good account.

Demonstrating Faith in Everyday Living/Sophie Allieu

In reading the word of God, we should often pause, to inquire of whom and of what the sacred writers' spoke; but especially our thoughts should be employed about the Redeemer. The Ethiopian was convinced by the teaching of the Holy Spirit, of the exact fulfillment of the Scripture, was made to understand the nature of the Messiah's kingdom and salvation, and he desired to be numbered among the Disciples of Christ. Those who seek the truth, and employ their time in searching the Scriptures, will be sure to reap advantages. The avowal of the Ethiopian must be understood as expressing simple reliance on Christ for salvation, and unreserved devotion to Him. Let us not be satisfied till we get faith, as the Ethiopian did, by diligent study of the Holy Scriptures, and the teaching by the Spirit of God; let us not be satisfied till we get it fixed as a principle in our hearts. As soon as he was baptized, the Spirit of God took Philip from him, so that he saw him no more; but this tended to confirm his faith. When the inquirer after salvation becomes acquainted with Jesus and his gospel, he will go on his way rejoicing, and will fill up his station in society, and discharge his duties, from other motives, and in another manner than heretofore. Though baptized in the name of the Father, Son, and Holy Ghost, with water, it is not enough without the baptism of the Holy Ghost. Lord, grant this to every one of us; then shall we go on our way rejoicing. Romans 10:9 *"If you declare with your* *mouth, 'Jesus is Lord', and believe in your heart that God raised Him from the dead, you will be saved." * (NIV)

Here are some Biblical instances to give us a better picture of **'faith with works'** according to Hebrews chapter 11:

"By faith Abel offered unto God a more excellent sacrifice than Cain, by which he obtained witness that he was righteous, God testifying of his gifts: and by it he being dead yet speaketh. Abel believed God was his all provider, the source of his blessing, his God, so he offered his sacrifice unto him by faith. I believe Abel must have been trusting God for something, he wanted to please his God with the best sacrifice so God being pleased, will bless him, will grant his heart's desires. So for God to move in your situation, you have to give a sacrifice that will move God that will please him.

By faith Enoch was translated that he should not see death; and was not found, because God had translated him: for before his translation he had this testimony, that he pleased God.

By faith Noah, being warned of God of things not seen as yet, moved with fear, prepared an ark to the saving of his house; by which he condemned the world, and became heir of the righteousness, which is by faith.

By faith Isaac blessed Jacob and Esau concerning things to come.

By faith Jacob, when he was a dying, blessed both the sons of Joseph; and worshipped, leaning upon the top of his staff. By faith Joseph, when he died, made mention of the departing of the children of Israel; and gave commandment concerning his bones."

Have you ever taken a step of faith in the midst of nothing? Like buying that college admission form for your child even when you know you can't afford the college fees?

There is an account of a family who had nothing to eat in the home. No money, no food stuff, but the mother, trusting God for provision washed her cooking utensils, pour water into the rice cooking pot and waited for God to make the provision. Well, her waiting was not in vain because they were blest with food items and some money hours later. God can do the same for you. If you believe!

TWO

HOW DO YOU KNOW YOU HAVE FAITH?
EVIDENCE OF FAITH

For one to have faith or live in faith is a personal decision or step. We all experience the evidence of faith individually.

Accepting Jesus Christ as personal Lord and Savior is one step. The book of John 3:3 (Holy Bible) - says: *"Jesus said unto him verily, verily, I say unto thee, except a man is born again he can not enter the kingdom of God."*

Having the Spirit of God is another step. You need to be born of water and of the spirit
"Jesus answered, verily, verily, I say unto thee, except a man be born of water and of the spirit he can not enter the kingdom"

John 3:5 (Holy Bible). A true believer of God must have the Baptism of the Holy Spirit.

"For John truly baptized with water but ye shall be baptized with the Holy Spirit not many days hence"
Act 1:5 (Holy Bible)

The spirit of God helped me to know I have faith by giving me an insight into Hebrews 11:1 that says: *"faith is the substance of things hoped for and evidence of things not seen"*. For the purpose of this book I define substance as an element, a composition, an idea, a feeling, a thought. So faith is an element, a composition, an idea, a feeling, and a thought of what you hope for. You hope to get a good job, a modest way of living, a need to be addressed. You believe that you will see what you hope for happening in your life. Like saying I believe in the scripture that says *"but my God shall supply all your need according to His riches in glory by Christ Jesus." (Philippians 4:19 -KJV)* therefore, all my needs will be met. That which makes you say that, is the evidence of faith you have. What is the proof that you believe and hope to see what you are not seeing now? **People cannot see through you to know that you have faith. It is what you say and do about what you have not seen, which you hope for, that makes people say or know that you have faith. The evidence! So you see, faith without works is dead.** Even if you purpose in your heart, think about it in your mind, believe and confess that God will supply your needs; that is not enough. People and you will only know that you believe in this scripture by your evidence. What is that evidence? It is how you show your trust in God, how you talk about your trust in God, your confession, your doubtless attitude, your patience to wait on the Lord.

When you are faced with a trying situation, let me say for example there is not a single dime on you (in your pocket or purse), yet you know you will "see" food to eat and will surely eat it. That is the proof/evidence of your faith. Knowing that you will eat even though you cannot afford the food and there is no other means to get it, all attempts you made to beg for assistance was futile, even though you have not seen the food. That thing which makes you believe, know and be very positive that you will not sleep hungry but will surely eat is your faith. People should see the evidence of your faith. Your faith should be evident. It is like the word of God that says *we are the light of the world.* **It is when you exercise your faith and then what you exercise your faith on, comes to pass, then you will start to understand faith better. You will know that faith is indeed something worth having.** So you cannot have faith without your life showing an evidence of someone who has faith. You have to show faith in the way you feel, the way you think. Show that the negative circumstances surrounding your life are not what God wants for you or you want for yourself. Talk to the situation you are facing in Prayer.

Say this prayer:

You …(name the situation - sickness, lack, limitation, unfruitfulness, stagnation etc.) I don't know where you came from but you are leaving this moment, you are powerless and there is no two-way about it, no option but to leave. I take authority over you through Christ Jesus my Lord and I command your hold upon my life to be loosed. I degree and declare that the end is now! Whatever legal grounds and stronghold you have, I disconnect and separate myself from it. My life is not a lab creature to be used for your evil experiments. I am made in the image and likeness of God. I believe in the death and resurrection of Jesus Christ of Nazareth, sanctified by His blood. I am a covenanted child of God. No weapon formed or fashioned against me shall prosper. From now onwards I am victorious in Jesus matchless and powerful name. Amen!

Now that you have said this prayer, you have no option but to believe. If you don't believe that God will take you out of that situation, then you are stuck with it; you will always experience that negative thing you have prayed for. That is not your portion. Continue to speak and confess the word of God upon your life. The devil is stubborn, be more stubborn than him and you will see what God will do in your life.

Faith is a fruit of the spirit *"But the fruit of the Spirit is love, joy, peace, longsuffering, gentleness, goodness, faith,"*[Galatians 5:22 - KJV]

You receive faith by the spirit of God - 1 Corinthians 12:9 (KJV) says: *"To another faith by the same Spirit; to another the gifts of healing by the same Spirit."*

The spirit of God is a teacher. Some people do not yield to the spirit. This is deliberate because they hold on to ungodly, sinful things and behavior. Some do not experience the presence of the spirit of God because they are so busy with activities of the world and desire to get rich and enjoy the pleasures of life; that they do not have time or make room for the things of God.

It is the spirit of God that builds ones faith. However, it also depends on how we avail ourselves for impartation. As an individual the word of God should be the lamp unto your feet. Walk in it always, all times.

Faith in God should be a MUST for every believer. Mark 11:22 (KJV) *"And Jesus answering saith unto them, have faith in God."*

"For we walk by faith, not by sight" 2 Corinthians 5:7

For You to Manifest Faith At All Times, For All Situations and Circumstances, You Should:

1. Yearn for it
2. Work on it
3. Believe in God
4. Trust in God alone
5. Allow God to have His way
6. You need to put in effort. That is, your faith should not be in words only but in action. Your mind, heart and body all synchronized in faith.
7. Ask God. Mathew 17:5 "And the apostles said unto the Lord, Increase our faith".
8. Never entertain doubt. Romans 14:1 "Him that is weak in the faith receive ye, but not to doubtful disputations."

"So whatever you believe about these things keep between yourself and God. Blessed is the one who does not condemn himself by what he approves."(Romans 14:22-NIV)

Evidence of your Faith is when:

I. You doubt not.
   Romans 14:23 "And he that doubteth is damned if he eat, because he eateth not of faith: for whatsoever is not of faith is sin".
II. Your faith stands in the power of God.
   1Corithians 2:5 "That your faith should not stand in the wisdom of men, but in the power of God."
III. You are faithful.
   1 Corinthians 4:2 "Moreover it is required in stewards that a man be found faithful."
IV. Your faith is not shaky/do not waver
   Hebrews 10:23 Let us hold fast the profession of our Faith without wavering; (for he is faithful that promised ;)James 1:6 "But let him ask in faith, nothing wavering. For he that wavereth is like a wave of the sea driven with the wind and tossed."

2 Corinthians 13:5 *"Examine yourselves, whether ye be in the faith; prove your own selves. Know ye not your own selves, how that Jesus Christ is in you, except ye be reprobates?"*

Demonstrating Faith in Everyday Living/Sophie Allieu

How Do You Tell Your Level Of Faith?

I hear there are levels of faith. Let me ask: Can faith be measured?

Two sisters were by the bedside of their mother, who had been sick and admitted for months; they were both attending the same Bible Believing Church and were born again Christians. Every morning they offered cooperate prayers for their sick mum, asking God to heal her. One day, their mother's health deteriorated and was rushed to the **Intensive Care Unit (ICU)**. They were both asked to wait outside whilst the doctor and others do their work.

Whilst they waited, the older sister asked the younger one that pray.

The younger sister responded by saying that she prefers her mother dies than go through all the sufferings she is experiencing now, and besides most people who are taken to the **ICU** rarely survive.

The older sister looked her boldly in the face and told her that she does not want her mother to die and left. She actually left to find a quiet place around the hospital compound to pray. She found a spot and spoke to God. Yes, she spoke and not prayed, because what she did was talking to God as if she was talking to someone standing in front of her.

She said: "God, I know who you are and what you can do, my sister says she prefers my mother to die than suffer in such a way. I equally do not want my mother to suffer, but I don't want her to die. She must not die, she will not die; God I see her face like that of a corpse. Her body lies motionless when I saw her last. The oxygen mask clung to her face. She could not breathe on her own, but for a life-supporting machine. God! make my heart to be at rest. I know you are going to heal her, but to save me from worrying unnecessarily, please give me a sign that she is going to make it, that she is going to live. Before this evening, let her get up from that sick bed on her own. This is what I ask of you my Lord, Amen!"

She joined her sister to wait. Three hours later a nurse ran towards them and told them that their mother had gotten up from the bed and had started walking around. The sisters leapt for joy and ran to see their mum. The older sister was just thanking and praising God for answering her prayer. The mother was transferred from the ICU, to a Ward so she could continue treatment. Five days later, she was discharged. It doesn't matter how badly the situation seems, God is never late, He is always on time. Our faith should be unwavering for God to move.

The Bible talks about level of faith several times by using the words **'increase'**, **'measure'** and **'As'**.

> *2 Corinthians 10:15 "Not boasting of things without our <u>**measure**</u>, that is, of other men's labours; but having hope, when your faith is <u>**increased**</u>, that we shall be enlarged by you according to our rule abundantly."*

> *Mathew 17:6 "And the Lord said, if ye had faith as a grain of mustard seed, ye might say unto this sycamine tree, be thou plucked up by the root, and be thou planted into the sea; and it should obey you."*

We can say there is level of faith because our faith needs to increase. We should work towards increasing our faith. The greater your faith, the bigger the manifestation of God's power. So increase your faith! And you will experience great move of God in your life.

An individual who desires to increase faith should:

I. Spend time reading the Bible. Studying the word builds your faith. Bible study should be paramount. You can join any Bible Study group for better enlightenment.

II. Personal quiet time brings you closer to God and understanding His words. Have time to pray and ask God to talk to you.

III. Be sensitive to the presence of the spirit of God in your life. You must be able to distinguish the voice of God. Always recognize the spirit of God and allow it to work in your life.

IV. Read Christian books and watch preaching video tapes

V. Desire it (faith), search for it, and practice it at tough times. Always listen to the Holy Spirit and do what He says.

VI. Focus on God when you are faced with problem, challenge, trials etc. tell God you rely on Him to take you out of it. Don't just say it. Mean it and do it.

VII. Always have the attitude of thanksgiving even before you receive your answered prayer.

THE FOUR 'TS' ARE SOME OF THE THINGS THAT COME OUR WAY:

1) Test of times
2) Trials
3) Temptations
4) Tribulations

Test of times: in this context is - hard times, test of faithfulness in God. Do we withstand the test of time by holding on to the finisher of faith or do we give up? Can you venture into the realities of what you are about to face due to a recent decision you took? For example you used to cohabit with your lover and becoming a born again requires the two of you to live in separate homes and your partner who gives you all the financial assistance refuses to oblige to your new terms of the relationship and threatens to end the relationship. Test of times! Will you withstand it and trust God or give in?

Trials: a difficult or annoying experience. It could be loss of a loved one, financial instability, loss of job or things you hold dearly and many other hardships. Have this in mind: *"consider it pure joy, my brothers and sister, when ever you face trials of many kind,"* (James 1:2 –NIV)

Temptations: the word has a sinister connotation in present day usage that is opposed to the original meaning of neutrality. Neutrality as in "putting to the proof" or the testing of character or quality; for instance Abraham was "tempted" when he was asked to offer Isaac as sacrifice. Let me hasten to say that it is one thing to be tempted and another thing to fall for or by that temptation. By conquering temptation, one may achieve a higher nobler level in faith and Christendom.

Tribulations: in other words -trouble or affliction of any kind; distress, trouble or persecution It denotes calamities.

How we respond to these things, determine whether we have faith in God or not. When some people face any of these, the first person they run to is their fellow man, meaning they believe man will solve their problems Another set of people will call on God – they will pray, embark on fasting, ask men of God and fellow Christians to pray for them, go through deliverance if possible. Some go to Juju/fetish priest and resort to all forms of diabolical means to proffer solution. Some experience prolong test of times, Trials, temptations and Tribulations.

A believer should expect the four 'Ts'. Being a "seasoned born again" Christian doesn't mean you will not experience them but by faith you overcome and even get a priceless reward.

1Peter 1:7 *"That the trial of your faith, being much more precious than of gold that perisheth, though it be tried with fire, might be found unto praise and honour and glory at the appearing of Jesus Christ:"*

CERTAIN ELEMENTS OF HUMAN MIND THAT INHIBITS DEMONSTRATION OF FAITH:

Doubt

I define doubt for the purpose of this writing as: ***knowing the truth and not believing it will work for us.*** We know God is a provider and protector yet in our actions and thoughts we don't fully trust Him to do it. We trust God to bless us, but we do not put our entirety into it. Our heart believes but our minds and actions waver and do contrary things. For instance, we trust God for a job but we have specific people in mind and things we do that we think can get us that job. Whom do you believe God or the person you think will get you the job?

We also limit God. We believe God can heal but the way we feel makes us do otherwise. We know and believe God can heal us but when pain is severe we take painkiller and when the painkiller does not work, we go back to God as our last resort. In another situation, there are people with little faith in God, who resort to diabolical means for cure and after several fruitless attempts they seek God for solution and He heals them. That is to tell us that God uses multiple ways to try our faith. He is always happy when after we have humanly tried and failed we resort to our Maker.

Sometimes we think too much, get worried too much. Believe that, the situation you find yourself in has not come to stay. It will pass off, relax your mind allow God to take full control.

When we say faith in action, we mean what we do should be in line with what we believe. You just cant say I believe God will heal me and then you say I will take medicine instead; that means you trust the medicine, even if you take the medicine, believe that it is God's power that works through the medicine. Act in faith, if you can't walk, get up and ask God to give you strength to do so. Trust God wholeheartedly.

How do you Handle Doubt

1) Trust in God fully, with your whole being

2) Listen to Him and act upon His instructions
3) Don't trust in the arm of flesh (man). "Woe to those who put their trust in man" Jeremiah 17:5
4) Confess Scriptures to yourself and the situation.
5) Remind God of His word
6) Remain focused on the Lord.

The Psalmist said: " I will lift up my eyes unto the hills, from whence cometh my help. My help cometh from the Lord, which made heaven and the earth. He will not suffer thy feet to be moved: he that keepeth thee will not slumber. Behold, he that keepeth Isreal shall neither slumber nor sleep. The Lord is thy keeper: the Lord is thy shade upon thy right hand. The sun shall not smite thee by day, nor the moon by night. The Lord shall preserve thee from all evil, he shall preserve thy soul. The Lord shall preserve thy going out and thy coming in from this time hence forth and even forevermore." (Psalm 121 – KJV)

Many a times, we are so drowned by and sunk in our misery that all we yearn for is pity from others and self-pity. That is what destroys a person.

It is better to trust in the Lord than to put your confidence in man. (Psalm 118:8 -KJV)

Brethren when you have faith, in other words trust in God, you have peace of mind. You experience a special kind of peace and contentment that you are worried about nothing.

Keep this in mind – James 1:6

"But when you ask, you must believe and not doubt, because the one who doubt is like a wave of sea, blown and tossed by the wind."

Fear

Fear is a weapon the devil uses to (quench) our faith.

The devil instills fear in us through various forms. Fear of going to die due to ill health or accident or threat from someone; fear of the night/darkness due to dreadful horrific experiences nightmares; fear of failure, fear of loosing a loved one, fear of change - positive change and fear of the future to name, but a few.

Let me share my experience with you. One night, at about 11pm, I started to feel some pain in my chest, my chest began to get tight and I left like my breath was beginning to get shallow. The way you feel when someone holds your mouth and nose at the same time. My breath began to seize. I became panicky and called a Pastor friend who told me to get a glass of water, he prayed and asked me to drink it; nothing changed. Infact my condition aggravated. I started praying and declaring: "I will not die but will live to testify the goodness of God." The truth is while I said that, I was filled with fear that I was going to die. Suddenly I had that still voice of the Holy Spirit saying to me: *the devil wants you to fear and is using that fear to overcome you. Don't be afraid be bold and be confident, war against him and you will overcome.* I stood up, braced myself with all the faith in me and started praying. I spoke directly to the devil and said: "listen to me devil, my God has just revealed to me your defeated trick, I know you want to use fear to overcome me and claim my life. Let me tell you that from now onward I will not fear any negative thing that comes my way because I know it is coming from a defeated fool". Brethren, immediately I confessed that, the power of God filled me, the pains disappeared I felt relieved and normal. I never had that experience again. It left me with boldness and fearlessness against the devil and knowledge of his vices.

Let me hasten to say here that the devil does not relent but by the spirit of God we will always overcome. Some two years after that experience, the devil attempted to build fear in me. I say my usual prayers every night. I mean prayer of protection (cover my compound, body soul spirit, my properties, my loved one friends and relatives that are not agents of darkness with the blood of Jesus and God to watch over all; commit my dreamland to God and ask God to fill me with the spirit to overcome in my dreams etc.). Despite all these prayer points I found myself looking towards the window to see if thieves have opened it, I started to fear that thieves will one day break into my house and attack me. Thank God for Jesus. This happened for some time and the spirit of God drew my attention to it. The spirit told me to allow my faith to penetrate my heart and mind. Meaning when I lay down to sleep, my heart should be at rest and I should relax my mind. The Holy Spirit told me that it is God's responsibility to protect me; mine is to sleep. That was it no more fears, I slept soundly ever since.

How to Handle Fear

1. Have a relationship with God
2. Receive the baptism of the Holy Spirit, born of the spirit
3. Allow your faith to penetrate your heart and mind
4. Be sensitive to the spirit of God. Listen and do what he says
5. Know your God and what He is capable of doing in your life. If you know Him as your protector, then believe that He will protect you.
6. In the midst of fear, confess the word of God to that situation
7. Put on the full armour of God so you can take your stand against the devil's schemes
8. Go into a spree of warfare when you sense fear. Be determine to overcome through Christ Jesus
9. Be mindful of the wiles of the devil

" Do not be afraid of what you are about to suffer. I tell you, the devil will put some of you in prison to test you, and you suffer persecution for ten days. Be faithful, even to the point of death, and I will give you life as your victors" (Revelation 2:10 –NIV)

"Do not fear, for I have redeemed you; I have summoned you by name; you are mine" (Isaiah 43:1). You are God's so do not fear.

Anxiety/Worry

The English Dictionary (offline 1.2.2) defines Anxiety as: "An unpleasant state of mental uneasiness, nervousness, apprehension and obsession or concern about some uncertain event. An uneasy or distressing desire (for something)…"

Most times in life, we are either eager to get something, or have a prayer answered and are most times impatient so much so that anxiety sets in. There is nothing good about anxiety. A Christian should not allow himself or herself to get to that state. Proverbs 12:25 say: "*Anxiety weighs down the heart…*" You see! Anxiety weighs down the heart; it brings sadness and discouragement.

How to Handle Anxiety

I. Be expectant in the Lord.

II. Meditate on His words always and confess scriptures that speak positively into your situation. Scripture like Isaiah 43:2-5:

"When you pass through the waters, I will be with you; and when you pass through the rivers, they will not sweep over you. When you walk through the fire, you will not be burnt; the flames will not see you ablaze.

For I am the Lord your God, the Holy one of Israel, your savior; I give Egypt for your ransom, Cush and Seba in your stead.

Since you are precious and honored in my sight, and because I love you, I will give people in exchange for you, nations in exchange for your life.

Do not be afraid for I am with you; I will bring your children from the east and gather you from the west..."

III. Let God be your consolation.

"When anxiety was great within me, your consolation brought me joy." (Psalms 94:19 -NIV)

IV. Say kind words to yourself and be around people who say kind words to you not those that will dampen your spirit. Proverbs 12:25- *"Anxiety weighs down the heart, but a kind word cheers it up."*

V. Dismiss Anxiety from your heart.

> *"So then, banish anxiety from your heart and cast off the troubles of your body, for youth and vigor are meaningless."*
> (Ecclesiastes 11:10 -NIV)

Worry

The same Dictionary defines worry as:

"Disturb the peace of mind of; afflict with mental agitation or distress.

To be troubled, to give way to mental anxiety."

This is what the devil does to our minds – "disturbs the peace" of our minds. Affliction is one of the strategies of the devil. It afflicts with "mental agitation or distress"; causing nervousness which is not good for the health of the body.

How to Handle Worry

1. Pray.

    The songwriter says: "why worry, when you can pray? Trust in Jesus and He will lead the way. Don't be like doubting Thomas but resting on His promise. Why worry, worry, worry, when you can pray"

2. Appreciate God for your body and especially your life.

    > *"Therefore I tell you, do not worry about your life, what you will eat or drink; or about your body, what you will wear. Is not life more than food, and*

>   the body more than clothes?" (Matthew 6:25-NIV)

3. Allow God to protect and defend you. Don't do it your way.

>   *Luke 21:14:"But make up your mind not to worry beforehand how you will defend yourselves."*
>   *Luke 12:11: "When you are brought before synagogues, rulers and authorities, do not worry about how you will defend yourselves or what you will say,"*

4. Stop worrying about your future and that of your loved ones. For the Bible says:

>   *"Therefore do not worry about tomorrow, for tomorrow will worry about itself. Each day has enough trouble of its own" (Matthew 6:34 – NIV)*

5. Always testify of God's goodness and believe that you will overcome by the blood of Jesus.

>   *"And they overcame him by the blood of the Lamb and by the word of their testimony; and they loved not their lives unto the death."*

THREE

TEST OF FAITH - Faith in action

BIBLICAL CASE STUDIES OF PEOPLE WHO PRACTICED FAITH

Abraham

"By faith Abraham, when he was called to go out into a place which he should after receive for an inheritance, obeyed; and he went out, not knowing whither he went.

By faith he sojourned in the land of promise, as in a strange country, dwelling in tabernacles with Isaac and Jacob, the heirs with him of the same promise:

For he looked for a city, which hath foundations, whose builder and maker is God.

By faith Abraham, when he was tried, offered up Isaac: and he that had received the promises offered up his only begotten son.

Of whom it was said, that in Isaac shall they seed be called:

Accounting that God was able to raise him up, even from the dead; from whence also he received him in a figure." **(Hebrews 11: 8, 9, 10, 17-19 KJV)**

The book of Romans accounted for Abraham in Chapter 4 verses 9, 12-14, 16, 19-22:

"Cometh this blessedness then upon the circumcision only, or upon the uncircumcision also? for we say that faith was reckoned to Abraham for righteousness.

And the father of circumcision to them who are not of the circumcision only, but who also walk in the steps of that faith of our father Abraham, which he had being yet uncircumcised.

For the promise, that he should be the heir of the world, was not to Abraham, or to his seed, through the law, but through the righteousness of faith.

For if they which are of the law be heirs, faith is made void, and the promise made of none effect:

Therefore it is of faith that it might be by grace; to the end the promise might be sure to all the seed; not to that only which is of the law, but to that also which is of the faith of Abraham; who is the father of us all,

And being not weak in faith, he considered not his own body now dead, when he was about an hundred years old, neither yet the deadness of Sarah's womb:
He staggered not at the promise of God through unbelief; but was strong in faith, giving glory to God;
And being fully persuaded that, what he had promised, he was able also to perform.
And therefore it was imputed to him for righteousness."

Sarah

"Through faith also Sarah herself received strength to conceive seed, and was delivered of a child when she was past age, because she judged him faithful who has promised
Therefore sprang there even of one, and him as good as dead, so many as the stars of the sky in multitude, and as the sand which is by the sea shore innumerable.
These all died in faith, not having received the promises, but having seen them afar off, and were persuaded of them, and embraced them, and confessed that they were strangers and pilgrims on the earth." (Hebrews11:11-13 - *KJV*)

Moses

"By faith Moses, when he was born, was hid three months of his parents, because they saw he was a proper child; and they were not afraid of the king's commandment.

By faith Moses, when he was come to years, refused to be called the son of Pharaoh's daughter;

Choosing rather to suffer affliction with the people of God, than to enjoy the pleasures of sin for a season.

Esteeming the reproach of Christ greater riches than the treasures in Egypt: for he had respect unto the recompense of the reward

By faith he forsook Egypt, not fearing the wrath of the king for he endured, as seeing him who is invisible.

Through faith he kept the Passover, and the sprinkling of blood, lest he that destroyed the firstborn should touch them.

By faith they passed through the Red sea as dry land: which the Egyptians assaying to do were drowned.

By faith the walls of Jericho fell down, after they were compassed about seven days.

By faith the harlot Rahab perished not with them that believed not, when she had received the spies with peace." (Hebrews 11:23-31 –*KJV*)

David

David was a shepherd boy who defeated Bears and Lions and by faith was able to defeat Goliath (a Philistine giant that threatened the lives of his kindred – the Israelite for forty days) with sling and a stone. He did not seem to have known what it was to be afraid. David never had the plan to or intention of fighting Goliath, he was asked by his father to take food to his brothers in the army camp. When he saw that the army of the Isrealites fled from the Philistine giant he asked who is this uncircumcised Philistine that he should defy the armies of the living God. In 1 Samuel 17: 37, David told Saul that: *"The Lord who rescued me from the paw of the lion and the paw of the bear will rescue me from the hand of this Philistine…"* (NIV). He made a declaration of faith to Goliath *"you come against me with sword and spear and javelin, but I come against you in the name of the Lord Almighty, the God of the armies of isreal, whom you have dified. This day the Lord will deliver you into my hands and I'll strike you down and cut off your head. This very day I will give the carcasses of the Philistine army to the birds and the wild animals, and the whole world will know that there is a God in Israel."*

Wow! What a show of faith by David.

1Sam22: 14 - Then Abimelech answered the king, and said, and who is so faithful among all thy servants as

David, which is the king's son in law, and goeth at thy bidding, and is honorable in thine house?

REAL LIFE TESTIMONIES/LIFE EXPERIENCES OF PEOPLE WHO PRACTICED FAITH

How we express our faith can only be determined by the prevalent circumstance or situation. Have you ever been in a situation where everything seems to fall apart? No source of income (joblessness, no business capital)?

There are times we wake up in the morning not knowing how we get meal for the day. There comes a time the needs of our family especially school and college fees of our children become humanly impossible to meet. The medication of a sick husband or wife demanding huge sum of money; or that house rent to pay; or that laon you took and the debtor is asking you to pay back.

Some people were willing to share their testimonies and life experiences in this book. Please read you will be blessed:

"My name is **Esther** I was the first to get married, have a first degree and post graduate degree in my family both Maternal and Paternal. All of these did not come easy. I was born to parents who were well placed, especially my father. He had big government position, head of a whole government department. He had fleet of vehicles; we lived in a house with a swimming pool and everything that goes with rich man's house. My mother was almost always travelling overseas so much so that most of our things, especially what we wore were gotten from overseas. There was a turn of events when I was twelve years old and in form two of secondary school. My father died and my mother fell ill; her condition deteriorated so badly that she was rushed to a nearby country for medication. I was stocked with my grandparents who were not on any form of earning. That was when I experienced and understood the true meaning of 'pangs of hunger'. I then knew what lack truly meant. Notwithstanding all of these, I was raised to be God-fearing and to trust in God. My grandparents were missionaries, needless to say the kind of spiritual regiment I must have be in. Years went by after my first degree, marriage and my post graduate degree, I opened a charity organization which flourished progressively for 8yrs. On the 9th and 10th years of operations funding was low until it stopped and organization was not functional. In the midst of all of these, my marriage went through tough times and I got separated from my husband, also developed female related health problem after a dream. Talking of which, the dream was really scary. Immediately I woke up the following morning I started experiencing severe stomachache and was rushed to a hospital, the Doctor recommended that my womb be removed. I stood up with authority as a believer, a child of God and said: no doctor of doom will tamper with me, the God whom I serve said I will be fruitful and multiply. He is more than able to handle anything that comes my way. This said, I got discharged and never went the doctor's way. About a month after, my relative a medical practitioner came to visit me and I narrated my experience at the hospital. The doctor in question was his colleague so he invited him over. The doctor denied doing such a thing. I put it to him that he wrote it on my bedside chart, which was checked and confirmed that indeed he recommended my womb to be removed (hysterectomy). Immediately he acknowledge and said he did not know what came over him because he will never in his right senses think of such a thing, as young as I am. Well, it goes without saying that it was a manipulation."

What I want you to gather from the above narration is the demonstration of faith by my sister. She spoke the word she believed and acted upon it. Imagine if she had succumb to the doctor's recommendation and gotten her womb removed under that high demonic manipulated time? How would she have felt when she would have realized that the doctor's decision was not just wrong out and of the ordinary, but was definitely not what God wanted for her? Brethren, this is how the devil works, so many lives and destinies have been destroyed as a result of lack of faith. Lack of faith and trust in God will lead to taking wrong decisions in life and doing things that are detrimental.

Here is another true-life experience:

"My name is Tony, when I completed college I had a lucrative job and I was able to save enough to start my own business. The business thrived so well, I was considered one of the millionaires in my town and was very popular until one day a particular guy came over to me and said people are bent on ruining my business, I told him my God will not allow them to succeed. The same guy went over to my cousin and said the same thing. My cousin came over to my office and I gave her the same response that my God will not allow such a thing to happen to me. I had a dream in which I saw my business certificate lying on a pavement with the writings on the certificate faded, especially the name of my business. A voice told me in the dream that this is what they want to see happen to my business; as the writings fade on the certificate, so will my business fade.
First thing in the morning, I went to see my Pastor to explain my dream. He went over to my business center,

prayed and anointed the whole place. He even prayed for my shop workers too. Months turned into a year and I saw my business collapse. Life became tough. I could not afford to pay rent for my business house. I sold my car to raise some money to build my business that too did not yield any fruit. I fasted and prayed. My prayer partners joined me in prayers yet things did not improve. I spent all my savings to save my business but everything went down the drain. It reached to a peek where I could not afford meal for my family not to talk of addressing other basic needs. A millionaire turned 'zeronaire' (zeronaire is a coined word to express the state I was reduced to. Zero financially) in the eyes of men. Thank God for Jesus because in Him I am rich. I serve a rich God. I am made in His image and likeness so I am rich! One day I sat my family down and told them the situation we were in, even though they realized what was going on. One thing I told them was: **it is not our responsibility to feed or clothe ourselves; it is God's duty and He will never fail.** I read Luke 12:22-28 to them:" *Then Jesus said unto the disciples: therefore I tell you, do not worry about your life, what you will eat; or about you body, what you will wear.*

For life is more than food, and the body more than clothes.

Consider the ravens: they do not sow or reap, they have no storeroom or barn; yet God feeds them: and how much more valuable you are than birds!

Who of you by worrying can add a single hour to your?

Since you cannot do this very little thing why do you worry about the rest?

Consider how the wild flowers grow. They do not labor or spin. Yet I tell you, not even Solomon in all his splendor was dressed like one of those.

If that is how God clothes the grass of the field which is here today, and tomorrow is thrown into the fire, how much more will He clothe you – you of little faith!" (NIV). I told them Jesus is not a man that He should lie nor a son of man that needeth to repent. His word is ye and Amen. God has been faithful we eat everyday. There is another experience I want to share. There was this day we had nothing to eat unto 6pm. I gathered my family and asked them to thank God and that they should not be worried, God will surely provide. One of my children doubted, so he went out to visit a friend. I knew he went to get something to eat. As God could have it, he did not succeed. He came back with his head bowed in shame. I smiled at him and told him to sit by me. As I was about to talk to him, my phone rang. A friend of mine called to say he has been thinking of me throughout the day but was busy, however he was on his way to my place. My friend came over and gave me the sum of one hundred thousand leones saying it was a small amount and I should please accept it. God is good! Alleluia! That's how I trust God every day of my life. I did everything humanly possible within the faith to bounce back. I applied for jobs, scholarships, business proposal, nothing positive came out of all. One day I sat and was meditating when I said to myself that it could be God has a plan for my life. I knelt and prayed and asked God to have mercy on me for going outside His plans, for stepping out of His will. I asked him to take over my life at this time of my nothingness and make me what he wants me to be. There had been sad moments. Moments when I wanted something and could not afford it. Moments when I could not fulfill my financial responsibilities as head of my home and to support the work of God financially like I used to do. It pained me to see others pouring money into the house of God and taking all my blessings. Yet I did the best I could physically in the house of God through my time, my energy, ideas etc. Today I am not a businessman as I used to be but God revealed a talent in me I never knew I had and has placed me in a celebrated class of elites in my country. Not to talk of the spiritual experiences I have. I have come to know God better. I experience a closer relationship with God. There are certain gifts of the spirits that manifests in my life. Today all I want is to work for God. I have contentment. I am at peace. Glory to God!"

This is our brother's experience in the Lord. It is only faith that got him that far, with all the experiences he had, suicide would have been on his mind but because he had Jesus, he could not fear, he could not worry. I want to introduce you to this Jesus incase you haven't met him or you do not know Him that well. He is the way maker, destiny changer, the miracle worker, promise-keeper who says He will never leave nor forsake His own. He is the impossibility specialist, the great provider, the great defender, the comforter, the God who never fails, our all in all. He is able to handle anything that comes your way; He is able to accomplish what concerns you today and He is able to make you what He wants you to be. Lean on Him; trust in Him and your life will be at peace, everything will work out well for you. Have faith in God, wonderful things will happen to you.

This is another true-life experience of faith.

"My name is Ngewoyeh I am 19 years old. As a sickle cell patient I got one of those serious crises with various complications. It started little by little with headache, dizziness, sever pain in the heart then it got so serious that I could bear it not more nor could it be managed at home. I had to be rushed to the hospital. On arrival, I was sent straight to the emergency resuscitation room and placed on oxygen and other things to stabilize me. The doctor that attended to me said that my case was very serious and was not going to make it except for God's intervention. As I heard that, I thought of my mum's promise to me telling me God is going to make me well; with that background I smiled at the doctor saying it is well, though he wasn't directly talking to me. God really proved himself that day because I was to be admitted immediately from the resuscitation but there was no need for that because God himself stabilized me and man did not have anything left to do. So I was allowed to go home and I went home feeling much better on that day. I believed that it was because I believed God to heal me that's why I was well. When I went home I was feeling ok until later at night I got a serious attack. This time it was so serious I couldn't breathe or do anything. I was limp in the feet. That night was the worst night of my life. It wasn't easy but God made it OK. I thought I wasn't going to make it through the night because of how I felt and what was happening around me. I managed to call my mum who encouraged me to trust God and prayed with me. After that I started confessing God's word and promises just as my mum told me to do whenever I could not handle the pain and God saw me through. In the morning He arranged everything so quickly I was taking to the hospital again. On reaching the hospital, which was full of people, we struggled for doctors to see me and I was feeling as if life was ebbing out of me. It took God's favor for the doctors to see me and start treatment. There was no bed available they had to lay me on stretcher to administer treatment. I was feeling restless and lifeless as I was placed on the stretcher. All I could remember was the oxygen mask been placed on my face and an injection given to me which I couldn't even feel. That was the last thing I remembered. Next thing, I saw myself in a strange place; a clear and open place with a straight bright light. The closer I got to the light, the brighter it became I could not see through it and I really wanted to. At that moment I heard a voice telling me to return to where I came from and that I should not be there, but I never wanted to leave that place because I had this urge to go towards the light so I kept on walking straight to the light then my head started spinning and I felt this force pulling me from the back I did not turn but continued walking backwards. I heard voices inside my head. All of a sudden I saw myself standing in the resuscitation room. My eyesight was blurred at first. Whilst standing, I could see myself lying on the stretcher. I walked closer to my body lying still with one of my hands dropping loosely off the bed. The doctor pressed a machine on my chest shaped like an electric iron. I stopped hearing the beep sound of the machine. I saw the doctor took the machine off; a nurse disconnected what was on my chested like cables with plaster. The doctor shook his head left to right as if something bad has happened to me, the nurse looked sad. I touched my hand and felt current like an electric shock all over my

body something strange happen everything went blank my whole body was stiff and I woke up. It all seemed like a dream. Something I can't comprehend nor explain up till now. Just after that I started hearing the beep of the monitor as if it was the sound that woke me up and I heard my grandmother said "oh thank God she's moved" at the same time nurses came to attend to me followed by the doctor who was like "aa na God o" and I asked him how was I doing he smiled and said " your condition is still serious u can't breathe properly so you'll still need to be here. And there I was not realizing the battle GOD fought for me and giving me a second chance. Every single minute in that hospital was a battle God fought using the level of my faith in him. Things got better, because I had full confidence and trust in God. The doctor said I had no pulse, a nurse said doctor's try but it is God that heals."
Hallelujah!!!

FOUR

GOD'S WORD AND PROMISES ON FAITH

God's words and promises are to keep your faith. Read the scripture below and claim them; confess them; believe in them and they will manifest in your life. Never forget that we have a Father (God) who neither fails nor tell lies.

> *God is not human, that He should lie, not a human being, that He should change His mind. Does He speak and then not act? Does He promise and not fulfill. (Numbers 23:19-NIV)*

Be patient for His word to come to pass in your life. Sometimes you see your world coming to a standstill, but always remember:

> *Heaven and earth will pass away, but my words will never pass away.(Mathew 24:35-NIV)*

THESE ARE HIS PROMISES FOR YOU IF YOU ARE FAITHFUL (in other words – have faith):

I. He will preserve you.

Psalm 31: 23 - "O love the LORD, all ye his saints: for the LORD preserveth the faithful, and plentifully rewardeth the proud doer."

II. He will protect you.

Psalm 101:6 –"Mine eyes shall be upon the faithful of the land, that they may dwell with me: he that walketh in a perfect way, he shall serve me."

III. You will be wise and restrained

Proverbs 11:13- "A talebearer revealeth secrets: but he that is of a faithful spirit concealeth the matter."

IV. You will be a rare gem. Precious

Proverbs 20:6 –"Most men will proclaim every one his own goodness: but a faithful man who can find?"

V. People will have confidence in you and run for help

Proverbs 25:19 –"Confidence in an unfaithful man in time of trouble is like a broken tooth, and a foot out of joint."

VI. You shall flourish with blessings

Proverbs 28:20 –"A faithful man shall abound with blessings: but he that maketh haste to be rich shall not be innocent."

VII. You become righteous

Romans 3:22 –"Even the righteousness of God which is by faith of Jesus Christ unto all and upon all them that believe: for there is no difference:"

Romans 4:5 –"But to him that worketh not, but believeth on him that justifieth the ungodly, his faith is counted for righteousness."

VIII. You boast in the Lord by faith

Romans 3:27 –"Where is boasting then? It is excluded. By what law? of works? Nay: but by the law of faith."

IX. You are justified

Romans 3:28 –"Therefore we conclude that a man is justified by faith without the deeds of the law."

Galatians 2:16 –"Knowing that a man is not justified by the works of the law, but by the faith of Jesus Christ, even we have believed in Jesus Christ, that we might be justified by the faith of Christ, and not by the works of the law: for by the works of the law shall no flesh be justified."

X. You have peace with God

Romans 5:1 –"Therefore being justified by faith, we have peace with God through our Lord Jesus Christ:"

XI. You have access into God's grace

Romans 5:2 –"By whom also we have access by faith into this grace wherein we stand, and rejoice in hope of the glory of God."

XII. You have the right attitude

Romans 11:20 –"Well; because of unbelief they were broken off, and thou standest by faith. Be not high minded, but fear:"

XIII. You work according to your measure of faith

Romans 12:3 –"For I say, through the grace given unto me, to every man that is among you, not to think of himself more highly than he ought to think; but to think soberly, according as God hath dealt to every man the measure of faith."

XIV. Your gifts manifest according to your proportion of faith

Romans 12:6 –"Having then gifts differing according to the grace that is given to us, whether prophecy, let us prophesy according to the proportion of faith;"

XV. You receive the blessings Abraham

Galatians 3:7 –"Know ye therefore that they which are of faith, the same are the children of Abraham."

Galatians 3:8 –"And the scripture, foreseeing that God would justify the heathen through faith, preached before the gospel unto Abraham, saying, In thee shall all nations be blessed."

Galatians 3:14 –"That the blessing of Abraham might come on the Gentiles through Jesus Christ; that we might receive the promise of the Spirit through faith."

XVI. You live by faith

Galatians 3:11 –"But that no man is justified by the law in the sight of God, it is evident: for, The just shall live by faith."

Galatians 3:12- "And the law is not of faith: but, The man that doeth them shall live in them."

Habakuk 2:4 –"Behold, his soul which is lifted up is not upright in him: but the just shall live by his faith."

XVII. You experience God's faithfulness everyday

Lamentation 3:23–"They are new every morning: great is thy faithfulness."

XVIII. You become faithful in all things

Luke 16:10–"He that is faithful in that which is least is faithful also in much: and he that is unjust in the least is unjust also in much."

Luke 16:12 –"And if ye have not been faithful in that which is another man's, who shall give you that which is your own?"

XIX. You are found blameless and receive the promise

Galatians 3:22–"But the scripture hath concluded all under sin, that the promise by faith of Jesus Christ might be given to them that believe."

Brethren, bear this in mind that you will be damned if you cast out your faith:

"Having damnation, because they have cast off their first faith."1Timothy5:12-KJV

And now I implore you with this, keep the faith, let your faith remain genuine

"Now the end of the commandment is charity out of a pure heart, and of a good conscience, and of faith unfeigned:"1Timothy 1:5-KJV

FIVE

BENEFITS OF HAVING FAITH

These are some of the benefits of having faith (scriptures are from KJV):

1) **Do great wonders and miracles**
   Act 6:8 "and Stephen, full of faith and power, did great wonders and miracles among the people"
2) **Purified heart**
   Act 15:9 "and put no difference between us and them, purifying their hearts by faith"
3) **Churches established in the faith, and increased in number daily**
   Act 16:5 "and so were the churches established in the faith, and increased in number daily."
4) **Righteousness of God revealed**

Romans 1:17 "for therein is the righteousness of God revealed from faith to faith: as it is written, the just shall live by faith"

5) **You become child of God**
Galatians 3:26 "for ye are all the children of God by faith in Christ Jesus"

6) **You receive salvation**
Ephesians 2:8 "for by grace are ye saved through faith; and that not of yourselves; it is the gift of God."

7) **The sick is being saved and sins forgiven**
James 5:15 "and the prayer of faith shall save the sick, and Lord shall raise him up; and if he have committed sins, they shall be forgiven him"

HOW TO LIVE YOUR LIFE DAILY BY FAITH

1) Be sober, grave, temperate, sound in faith, in charity, in patience. Titus2:2
2) Listen to God the spirit of God and it must be strongly manifested in you. Be sensitive to the voice of "God. Study the way He communicates with you. He might not have one fixed way to talk to you but He sure has ways he communicates with you often, most frequently. God could speak through dreams, visions, and revelations. Sometimes you just sense it, it comes like an intuition. One thing is for sure. God confirms whenever He speaks. Could be through a sermon, radio message, a home visitation by a believer, counseling time with your pastor, through scriptures, songs and sometimes in a still soft voice; the list goes on.
3) Look unto Jesus as the author and finisher of your faith. Hebrews 12:2
4) Study the word of God and confess it
5) Pray without ceasing. Ask the Holy Spirit to teach you how to build on your faith.
6) Walk with the Holy Spirit

7) Be attentive and eager to hear from God.
8) Meditate on the move of God in your life and hold firm to those memories because the working of your faith produces perseverance (patience). James 1:3
9) Stand fast in the faith, and be strong and sober
10) Take the shield and put on the breastplate of faith
11) Be focused on what you seek the face of God for. Don't be distracted. Have no doubt
12) Look unto God and not what is happening around you.
13) Don't limit God. Think big. Ask big.

When you practice this, your faith would grow/increase in such a way that all it demonstrates is fearlessness, complete reliance in God and strong conviction that there is nothing God can't handle. You worry about nothing and fully confident that God is in control. You would see yourself yielding to His direction on how your life is run. You walk under the full leading of the Holy Spirit. You no longer own yourself, you see life differently, you would not be mindful of material things (you are content). You live to please God and not man.

Everyone has something s/he is trusting God for. No matter how rich, comfortable, poor or accomplished you are, there is always something you lack, and something you pray and ask God for. It doesn't matter what that thing is, live one day at a time in faith. Look unto God. Stop being desperate. Desperation leads to temptation. It is not bad to be determined in the positive sense of the word. Believe in that particular word of God that speaks about your situation. God knows it all. For you to have a quick breakthrough don't be greedy in trusting God. Don't ask for so many things at the same time. Take one specific thing you want God to handle before you go to the next.

Make sure what you are asking God for is according to His will. For instance when you ask God for a child know that for you to have the fruit of the womb is the will of God. So also are our needs; He said "I will supply your needs according to my riches in glory'. Stop worrying. You can't trust God and worry at the same time. Stop thinking how you can help yourself get what you want. If you do, you are making a big mistake and there is all likelihood that you are stepping out of God's will. Most times such actions lead to evil paths, sin and backsliding.

Remain composed and focused on your faith in Christ. Your heart should be at peace. Be sensitive to the voice of God and obey whatever He tells you(the previous chapters have dealt with some ways on how God speaks to you), be patient - Wait!

Your faith should be like the food you eat, the clothes you wear which you couldn't go without for a single day. God is loving, compassionate and caring. He does not want to see us unhappy. Whatever negative experience we have has a root cause. Ask the spirit of God to open your eyes to the cause(s) and when He does, ask him to direct and lead you through your deliverance. He sure will!

Take the risk. Some people know what it means to obey His word and do His will; but some don't because they fear what they will lose. For example A girl having an affair (committing fornication) with a man that pays her bills and addresses other needs will on the one hand want to obey God and other hand fear of losing her source of livelihood. This is ridiculous, there is no two-way about it because God is your source. Why not get from the true source directly because God gives a total package, customized package for you. It is good to always think outside the box and look at the bigger picture.

Remember the devil manipulates minds through doubts; fear, unbelief etc. Do not give heed to negative thoughts. Brush them off your mind when they come. Always have a positive mindset believing the battle is the Lord's and He will deliver you.

Finally Brethren, from child hood you have known or heard the holy scriptures, which are able to make thee wise unto salvation through faith which is in Christ Jesus. **Accept Jesus in your life and let Him take control.**

I leave you with the words of this song:
"So, amid the conflict whether great or small, do not be discouraged God is over all; count your many blessings angels will attend, help and comfort give you to your journey's end".
" Count Your Many Blessings" (Rev. Johnson OatmanJr/E.O. Excell)

Fight the good fight of faith, lay hold on eternal life, whereunto thou art also called, and hast professed a good profession before many witnesses. God bless you!

www.ingramcontent.com/pod-product-compliance
Lightning Source LLC
Chambersburg PA
CBHW031418040426
42444CB00005B/627